CLOSE ENCOUNTERS
Down Home

poems by

Pamela Yenser

Finishing Line Press
Georgetown, Kentucky

CLOSE ENCOUNTERS
Down Home

*This book is dedicated to Kelly, Jessup, and Becca Yenser
and
To the magic of family circles and crop circles everywhere*

*I write only because there is a voice within me
that will not be still....*

~Sylvia Plath—Letters Home

Copyright © 2021 by Pamela Yenser
ISBN 978-1-64662-434-8 First Edition
All rights reserved under International and Pan-American Copyright Conventions. No part of this book may be reproduced in any manner whatsoever without written permission from the publisher, except in the case of brief quotations embodied in critical articles and reviews.

ACKNOWLEDGMENTS

I wish to thank the editors and judges of publications in which these poems first appeared:

200 New Mexico Poems: an online anthology, First Sighting
Adobe Walls #2 Anthology of New Mexico Poetry:
    In the Garden of Demented Parents
Adobe Walls #3 Anthology of New Mexico Poetry: Lover Men
Bosque Press #9: Like Emily They shut me up in Prose
Connotations Press /An Online Artifact: First Sighting
IthacaLit: Damn, *il pleut* (Lauren K. Alleyne Difficult Fruit Prize)
Fugue: On the Road with Howdy Doody (Fugue Award)
Massachusetts Review: Finding Her Brother Lost & Zipper Trip
Nightbomb Review #2: Abduction (Nightbomb Press, Portland, OR)
Shenandoah: "A Dance for Mother"
W.B. Yeats Society of NY: To Mary Shelley, Regarding Monsters (Award)
Wichita State University Shocker Shock Art Summer, The End of TV
Witness Magazine: Snow Angels (Poetry Awards Finalist)

Publisher: Leah Huete de Maines
Editor: Christen Kincaid
Cover Art: Terry Gloeckler
Author Photo: Jon Kelly Yenser
Cover Design: Elizabeth Maines McCleavy

Printed in the USA on acid-free paper.
Order online: www.finishinglinepress.com
        also available on amazon.com
        and through Ingram at your local bookstore.

Author inquiries and mail orders:
Finishing Line Press
P. O. Box 1626
Georgetown, Kentucky 40324
U. S. A.

Table of Contents

- Like Emily They shut me up in Prose 1
- Close Encounters 2
- First Sighting 3
- Abduction 4
- The Awakening 5
- Finding Her Brother Lost 6
- On the Road with Howdy Doody 8
- Death Valley to Albuquerque on Route 66 10
- The End of TV 11
- A Dance for Mother 12
- Mother Nature 14
- Zipper Trip 15
- Memory's Gate 17
- Snow Angels 19
- In the Garden of Demented Parents 20
- Our Lives Were Like Firefly Light 21
- To Mary Shelley, Regarding Monsters 22
- Lover Men 25
- Damn, *il pleut* 26
- About the Cover Artist 33
- About the Author 34
- Praise for *CLOSE ENCOUNTERS Down Home* 35

Like Emily They shut me up in Prose

when I stopped   time Stood still
as multi-coated   children climbed
aboard the Preschool Bus.   I felt
the crash their mothers did not see
my Brain exploding like midnight
under a blinking colander of Stars
a substitute teacher   in my mirror
apologized for my totaled trunk
her perfect MAGA Suburban   left
unscathed   while I sat Dumb-struck
no Common Sense nor wits about me.

—Pamela Yenser (2014 Car Crash TBI)

Close Encounters

You're in that saucer
spinning over Roswell
on edge like a dime

You're no longer four
in the backseat of a car
holding your new brother

sharp as saucer wreckage
breathing in silver knives,
bodies of crumbled rock,

In a magic card trick
now you see it now you don't
Tighten your cold seatbelt

Close your eyes—you're high
like Father's borrowed aircraft
with flapping silvery wings

So long as you can survive
you won't forget the sunbaked
cloud angels airdropping you,

as your beating heart flew
before you in amazement
from heaven to home

Because that's what poets do

First Sighting

That day was the closest I've come to dying.
Father borrowed an airplane and flew us too close
over the glitter of balloons and kites, the ghost
of some tinfoil contraption or mylar "flying

machine." Everyone talked about the headline
in Roswell's *Daily Record* July 8, 1947—first
citing! It happened before my brother's breech birth
(cord-wrapped, high forceps). That disk made a beeline

along the same farms that Roswell's teen Rat-Pack
drove like hell through—"Hub" Corn and Ragsdale—places
right out of the show *Scariest Police Chases*.
"Their blood's as black as tar," reported Cactus Jack.

That thought of those burnt bodies whisks me in a dream
from the present to that past New Mexico town
where you, like a baby-faced moon, hung upside-down
circuitous with flashing eyes, have come to beam

me up again. I called you first a shooting star
or bad weather balloon made out of Kryptonite
but the crazy way you zoomed from then to tonight
makes me wonder now, brother, where the hell you are.

Abduction
~After William Carlos Williams' "Nantucket"

Glitter dust and cotton-
wood seeds trapped

against the front screen—
Storm cellar open—

Evidence of broken saucers—
On the bedside

stand, a pineapple
ruffled doily—and in

a mason jar, your missing
neighbor's chattering teeth.

The Awakening

> *She wanted something to happen—something, anything.*
> *She did not know what.* ~Kate Chopin, *The Awakening*

How many airplanes will it take
        to cure Father's flying mania?
A sudden opportunity
        transports us to California.

Where's Father anyway? A-ways
        across the beach, probably catching
up on airplane loads, inventing
        some secret Army flying machine

I still see him, the *LA Times*
        across his boxers, a flapping tent
of secret codes—information
        I cannot know, being innocent.

And where's Mother? She's putting pins
        in foam rollers, tanning in the nude
swimsuit bought to disappear in.
        In this scene, I can't find my swim tube

and Mother's sad—it's "postpartum"—
        maybe it's the news she shares
from the doctor. She will not hear
        of it. In her church of folding chairs

there's no cure but what the chosen
        ones choose. No choice but what the chosen
ones hope for—no hope for the lost
        except what is meant to be—through prayer.

No mom wants to be remembered
        For the things she didn't do—the gate
she left unlocked, the bedroom doors
        she didn't listen through, unheard cries,
untaken drugs he had to take.

He won't stay put. I tell him, "Stay"
        but he won't. Guess he was born that way.

Finding Her Brother Lost

Cooped up in a car. Damp cave.
Cat. Rat. Primitive words like sticks
to draw on the glass. Insects tap back,
tripping fluorescent switches.

Her mother says wait until
he is found—I can still hear her.
Helpless words. Watch them evaporate
like circles on a mirror.

She knows a story from church,
how the prodigal son finds
himself lost. Overhead, the moon's shirts
change like Mother changes his,

one after another, clinging,
tissue thin, clouding his face,
thrown in with the towels and wringing
out into one long milky way.

Wait and wait. Pick the scratches
his nails make, purple bracelets,
sad crescent moons rough as a surgeon's
stitches. Wait. Not saved yet?

Prodigal. You prod. I go.
Was it always in the cards?
High forceps going low.
Were the doctors playing God

to save him as (they'd said)
a vegetable—retarded? Picture
a potato. He climbed the fence
of the garden. Disappeared.

Was it not a miracle
a child could get so far?
Rattlers slide through the vegetal
fence. Further, there is water.

Slogging through oatmeal and cream
mush, he imitates that sound,
hands and knees plopping, algae green.
His diaper sinks like a stone.

Beginner's luck—he is fished
out and carried to her window
in Mother's arms, wet and washed
out—milquetoast, cold potato, fool

albatross, he quivers weightless
to her lap. She was born to be
protector of the innocent.
She is her brother's keeper.

On the Road with Howdy Doody

i.

Try it again, Brother. Death Valley.
We're going to take the short cut.
Say it. Death. *Debt. Debt. Debt.*

It's 1951—year of the black Lincoln
and Father's gangrenous appendix.
For me and my little retarded brother

childhood was a pink California stucco
and a couple of aces clothes-pinned
to our spokes *plak plak* down Coldbrook.

Broke as all get-out and low on brakes,
we made for Kansas in four long days,
each warm sunrise a punch in the (f)ace,

each hairpin-curve a tighter loop of knots:
not a touch of Tangee or taste of beer,
Hopalong, Wild Bill, or Howdy Doody.

Out with the old says our New Testament.
Off with news. It's the work of the devil.

ii.

Witch-eat-a. Air Capital of the world
says Father unfolding a map.
Kansas is where your mother and I met.

I like the strange sound of it. *Witch-eat-a,*
I say to Brother, biting back.
God turns the road ahead into water.

The water's boiling in my cloth canteen.
Its cool cap and chain comfort me.
Witch-eat-a. Say it after me. *Itch-Itch.*

We're taking my brother to the famous
Instant Truth of Logopedics
or something in that neighborhood. Looking

back, we might as well be abducting him
to outer space or heaven's gate
through which our mother keeps on praying us.

Father is pretending not to hear it.
He'd rather be engineering
thing-a-ma-jigs that can fly without wings.

He tapes them into circles of vellum
or foils of al-u-min-ium.
Say it after him, Brother: *Umm. Umm.*

Death Valley to ABQ on Route 66

We're pulling an old Airstream—
a silver bullet on wheels.
My parents are good looking
like Desi and Lucy when
they made *The Long Long Trailer*.
We have one catastrophe
after another—Mother
stabs herself with an ice pick
chipping ice between her legs
for the air conditioner
Father's made of sheet metal
a hamster wheel and a pull chain.
We're nearly to Needles when
we all smell it—asbestos!
That's when Brother gets ahold
on me and Mother begins
chanting the Lord's prayer again.
Once Route 66 crosses
itself, we all start peering
through the electric darkness
for our motel with a pool
at the neon diving sign
of a lady bent in two.

The End of TV

Before our Dark Ages
my brother and I watched it
where it sat oblately on its rag rug,
rabbit-ears quivering above the head of old
Chief Gray-face humming a nuclear test tune.

What happened next took a leap of faith as faint
as the warmed-up weather map of heaven's face:
where there was a warning, Mother heard it
and come it did—a purple wall cloud,
lightning, hail, the whole shebang
banging like a long train coupling.

It's coming, the newspaper confirmed—
so, Mother canceled the paper with a warning
shot over our bowed heads: *These are the last days
of dancing, books, TV, and news*—whatever that is.

I couldn't have been more than seven. I couldn't have been
more astonished if Desi and Lucy and Mr. Magoo himself
were bundled into a whirlwind or a biblical burning bush
and tumbled with us and the Lone Ranger and Tonto
through rough footage of Kansas Flint Hills, past
graveyards of stick and stone, on the shortcut
that spring took—that time through us.

A Dance for Mother

At nine I learned to love an image or dance,
wonderful fiction, when visions of the devil
made you tithe, trade in the family silver
and fast on water. Kept by an empty glass
and locking the bedroom to keep me outside,
you fastened heaven with a knot of hair.

I spun away, all petticoats and hair
loosened by the sway and pivot of my dance.
Suddenly seeing all, bent on the glass,
you caught me drawn beside
a window, looking at the moon in silver,
taught me a song to scare away the devils.

You say they take no wives, but how could the devil's
third of angels imitate your disarray of robes and hair,
flutter such a wound sheet, invent such a dance
to equal that reflection I saw blown in glass—
a shapeless couple moving side by side
inside the margin of their nervous silver.

The door's edge slipped away, a sliver
of light or air, a blade sharp as glass.
Looking, I left and felt it touch my hair.
All night I dreamed I tried that dance
until I knew a voice like the devil's
pounding the chambers I fancied inside.

You must have known, taking me to your side,
infinite verses, suspended dull silver
bridges: we must not mind the devil
but bend our knees and tuck away our hair
and try to sing though we may never dance.
Yet, when I sing my song turns into glass

before my eyes, an oval looking glass
with burning candles mounted either side,
near the face, burnishing the perfect silver.
I think it is the lake and center of the devil.
Letting down my robe and then my hair,
out into that haunted space I dance
      from side to side, new Alice in her glass,
      fly out the silver splinters of my hair.
      I am the devil. Watch me dance.

Mother Nature

My destiny, as far as I could see
        was flat—one gigantic piecrust baked
until it cracked and (grass)hoppers escaped

with a ratcheting chirr of legs, a (c)lick
        like mixer blades in a Pyrex bowl—
or the tick of Mother's Singer "serging"

back green bands the Dust Bowl cicadas ate.
        Above the whirl, cumulus piled up
in thick tornadic pads of hooks and eyes.

Who could I turn to? Mother Nature? She
        choked my brother with a natal cord.
The brain is not like a Mimosa tree—

a plant so tuned to (hu)man touch and light
        her spine's a bundle of nerves   which   cut
or winterkilled   multiplies underground.

In the springtime of my yard she (re)turns
        feathered in leaves compound and (d)angling
with pink earrings. She is called Wooly Bush

Silk Tree   Siris   Sirius the Dog Star.
        She is our best-tressed survivalist—
Miss(ed) Medusa of the vegetable world.

Zipper Trip

You do not pull my yellow hair
but tutor your retarded son to touch
    you know where.

With mouthy women you assert
your authority with belt and brush.
    I raise my skirt.

You mastermind such tricks, saw me in two
halves—the me watching the me washing
    Mother who

miscarries. Will she ever rise to speak
from this pool of fetus flesh and blood,
    phoenix weak?

In her state of mind, she'll never guess
what you'd like to do to us
    (you creep, you caress)

such as climbing into children's beds,
snatching wrists in human bracelets
    (this turns my head)

until you've half pressed nail-bitten lips
into wine. Once you take me on a trip
    back East, your hand

high on my thigh. In green cloverleafs
the wail of Pennsylvania Turnpike sirens
    (Stop! Thief!)

pull you over for crossing the dividing line—
hypnotic yellow highway ribbons.
    "How you doin'?" Fine?

"Licenses please. This is your father?"
He thinks I'm someone else's goddamned
      runaway daughter?

"How old are you, young lady?"
The blue serge arm of the law
      is rough and ready.

"I'll be sixteen." And will I ever
live long enough to trust myself
      with you? Never!

Is that all I have to say? To sign?
To make things right, do I lay it on
      the line or lie?

What's the charge at your tollbooth
this time? I can backslide, write nothing
      here's the truth:

not your silence fostered for twenty years
which speeds me madly down this freeway,
      not your cashmere

present to try on for size, a tight red wool
sheath with teeth, the slide of that back zipper
      you love to pull.

Memory's Gate

At home today, I'm pulling fence posts.
                I find this final tug at the truth,
two rows of four-by-fours in concrete
                hurts most; but isn't this work
to fix the boundaries of our home
                work we poets have got to do
if only to claim our safe place?
                As I push the final rotten post
back and forth, it gives way
                to truth, the pain of it pulling me
out by the root of memories
                deep as the nerve of a tooth.
The past is a trap the Jaws of Life
                can't break. Father's come unhinged
like a gate. He's undone the hook.
                What is left for me to do? I swing
from revelation to dumb denial
                from reality to dreams—of things
I can't touch so much as touch on
                can't change so much as be
changed by. I find this final tug
                at the truth of it hurts the most.
But isn't this the work, as I said,
                a poet's meant to do? If only we
could be normal. If only...what?
                If only there weren't this family
history slamming the lid on truth.
                Just as I'm finding these pickets
all too familiar, it comes to me....
                This is the height of the first
fence Father built to keep his boy
                safe at home in my company.
The width of the white rail I walked
                when Father lifted me in my skirt.
This is the first and last fence

                    to mind, the last old stake to pull,
The final gate to bad memories
                    I'll ever have to push through.
I put my back to it, and it opens.

Snow Angels
~For my Kansas brothers and sisters

It is our father who harries us
        along that old game of fox and geese.
                Our spokes creating an enormous
                      sign of peace

until we are chased until all fall down
        to make hourglass waves of skinny arms
                and spraddled legs becoming frigid
                      snow angels.

Decades later in a cold study
        I turn the flood lights on new snow
                alighting and arising like a memory
                      pillow fight:

                        crow's-nest flakes fall from the umbrella
                of night emptying their star-pierced
        shapes strained through a colander of light
manna bright

                    forming this illusion that I have
                traveled state to state and flake by flake
        backward through memory to myself
conceived back

                    then and there in a dormitory
                meant for students in a Midwest mining
        town where the military marriage
of a nurse

                    and her captain came undone and I
                vanished inside—becoming nothing
        more than desire in her lover's eyes
for a girl.

In the Garden of Demented Parents

Everything abandoned comes alive
nerve and nerve-end (de)signed to revive

and grow like topsy   without parents
nor any (ap)parent deterrents

to survival, replicating D-
N-A by magic   levitating me

above this state, held tight by sleight
of hand or eye   Houdini-like   the fright

of us trembling hares to the nuisance
of seventeen-year locusts   rude music

to our ears   earth's (re)tired planters panting
spring's softly seasoned song   implanting

in us seeds of what we ought to say
though we didn't say squat that day

in the lettuce, spinach, and carrots
in the garden of demented parents

lop-eared   loping, pink skin and baggage
plastered with patches of purple cabbage.

Our Lives Were Like Firefly Light

Caught in a jar, we lit up the night.

How did our collectors punish us?
Did Mother bruise us with brushes?

Did Father grow closer by inches?
Had he grown too big for his britches?

Was he mad enough to break into
her closet and remove each left shoe?

The lawyers said she had dementia.
Who was crazier was the question!

Leave, my darlings, that long-ago life
where Father knocked with a kitchen knife

at your side door. Shake off that old shoe-
stealing monster. I never left you

alone to remember. Now you're free
of Mary and the *Frankenstein* she

married. Look! I have razor blades sewn
into the hem of every poem.

To Mary Shelley, Regarding Monsters
*~With thanks to Leslie McGrath (June 15, 1957- August 7, 2020)
for her 2019 "Note of Pleasure."*

Was it a waking dream you had of *him*?
I've read your *Frankenstein* to take a look
at visionary art—its nuts and bolts.

How well we love that beast, technology.
"What is this sweet machine called modern man?"
We ask. "Where is that monstrous heart of him?"

The answer's in his zippered face and pants
and in his blessed Doppelgänger-ness—
a mirror that won't let him see beyond

himself, his nature's beaten path to God.
As new viruses project themselves into
relationships of love (postmodern love)

our DNA becomes a brave new world:
a microcosm and homunculus—
man's tiny self at work in every cell.

When you take pen and paper to your bed
your thoughts belie the bellow of the soul
that sets your sail. What would you say?

It's written in your book of days…and nights:
*I did not sleep, nor could I be said to think;
My imagination…guided me…I saw….*

What could you see? What Dr. Frankenstein
through scientific methodology would see.
That horrid thing, you say, *That odious work*

of love that begs for life—these monsters we
have hid beneath our beds, or up a sleeve,
or in the beating closets of the heart.

I see them still; you write, *the very room, the dark
parquet, the closed shutter, with the moonlight
struggling through and the sense I had.* You had?

Of what? *Realities,* you said, of lust.
Despite your mother's feminist tracts,
your father's literary world is severing

you from those who serve and wait, a Siamese
of sorts, your lust inseparable as Eve
from God's mistake. And thus, your work began.

You started where you could. At birth. A month
to be recounted. November what? *Sixteenth?*
Then happy birthday to Frankenstein and me!

I began that day with the words, you wrote,
It was a dreary night of November.
(An echo from Keats' "Sleep and Poetry.")

You woke in terror of the tale you'd tell
yourself, not knowing day from night, your mind
the horrid thing itself, your Frankenstein.

And mine. As Godwin goaded you with cold
and calculating mind, so Father furthered mine,
muck-mastering away my college funds.

Your father's love was deep and *half-obsessive.*
Those words you chose! No wonder when I read
your *Frankenstein*, I saw my father drawn.

And so, we married poetry and took its name
for better or for worse—but worse than what?
Some unions have a way of turning thoughts

to thugs, long lines of monsters begotten
(in the biblical sense): some great and some
forgotten, some in part and some in full,

fractals of originality—the coupled male
and female parts a match, Ovidian;
or Dante-esque, with interlocking limbs.

Don't mind me. My mind's a fractured Arne,
that river Frankenstein would thrash to reach
his *Mer de Glace*, the mirror of himself.

My Charon is the Cripple Creek I cross.
I try to heal myself through Blake and Frost,
to find some common cure in fire and ice—or verse.

But even as I type, some monster takes
a hand, spell-checking *Blanc* to Blanch and
transmogrifying my last name to "Answer."

The ghost in the machine is ours, not Frankenstein's.
We're streaming lines of blood to save ourselves
and blaming man. I write you more than Moore

or Yeats might say, but less than Olds and Plath—
without whose frank confessions, who would know
the depths to which a woman sinks each day?

Lover Men

I'm exchanging words this fall
with old boyfriends. "Don't call

me—I'll email you," I say when
addressing my brave gentlemen

callers from our college years.
Should I tell them their careers—

department heads, ambassadors—
put me in mind of paramours

with rescissions? My lover back
in Kansas tracks Iraq attacks.

Can he track me? Can't say I'm mad
about the prospect of my failing dad

who stalks me in his underwear—
old Fruit of the Loom. I'm elsewhere

now. He's driving me to liquor
just by pointing out his dick or

scar. "It's a small thing," I should say
and turn and look the other way

but aren't dads monstrous in that state
whether average or great?

Damn, *il pleut*

i.

I'd like a father—but, goddamn,
we're so over. I was less than

one when my mother and I flew
across the Atlantic to you.

Mother was a nurse, nursing me
on empty. Eggs cost real money

and the Army didn't bother
to put up your wife and daughter.

Padre di ciao! High in a flat
in Cortina, you pinched your hat

into a (tri)angle. Your hair
was debonair and black. I swear

I've forgotten the rest, except
the iron bed where we three slept…

and me on a sled in the snow.
being pulled by a dog I don't know.

You took a prize-winning picture.
I think it captured my future

survival: flying in defense
of you by the seat of my pants.

ii.

In Roswell, you flew us over
the saucer wreckage. Whatever

the aliens brought was a curse
on us—the unfortunate birth

of my brother who could not talk.
You might say his life was a wreck

from which we never recovered
and mother never said never

until I had to save myself
by telling on you. Nothing else

to do, with two little sisters
and a brother in our pastor's

hiding place. I got out of (h)arm's
way by falling into the arms

of the writer you tried to get
(d)rafted. Though we weren't married yet

we were living together when
the draftboard told us of that scam.

What kind of dad does that? You called
to try and get my boyfriend killed?

iii.

In Washington, we stood in line
against the war in Vietnam.

In Oregon, trees turned to logs,
and clouds to raining cats and dogs.

Grandkids went from school to college,
Your son's son mentioned marriage,

and your daughter's call returned
a letter! Our (b)ridges aren't burned?

After your silence, I feel hope
in this Pandora's envelope...

or money? (N)ope! Only talk of it,
as if that matters. More bullshit:

Do I have an IRA account? No!
You stole my savings long ago

before you managed to harass
my husband's draftboard and my boss.

You can't imagine what you've missed:
(grand)children you haven't kissed.

Unlike your children, they feel safe.
I have pictures you didn't take.

iv.

I have a husband whose concerns
match mine. He studies and discerns

that love is not demanded nor
(with)held for twenty years or more.

We've been escaping overseas:
England, France, Spain, Italy, Greece.

Armed Colonels marched into a play
at Epidavros. I learned *Nai*

means yes, and a nod means no. When
did no ever mean yes instead?

Bonjour, mon père. We've gone to Rennes.
But, damn, *il pleut!* We're back again

in Oregon to find what things
we've lost. This paradox has wings.

The more we fly, the less distance
we gain. It's that bright red (lip)stick

of memory. The more I write
my past, the more it line by line

takes me home into that summer
Daddy wrote "Whore!" on my mirror.

v.

You'll never find me here. The neck
of Idaho is steep, and like

in Italy, above the heel.
Up here, I have a chance to heal.

Here, you can't spank—or zip my dress.
Palouse Hills are blown from the loess

of volcanic dust, not the live
mouth of Vesuvius you dived

into with those generals—those who
trusted you. What would you *not* do?

I'm starting my own war, *mon père*.
Why were we afraid? You were there.

Why am I obsessed with books and sex?
Stressed about abuse? Plath (di)stressed?

Drawn to martyrdom? Joan of Arc?
Christ, why do I write in the dark?!

From the safety of my armchair
I scan my *New Yorkers* for their

accounts of war: the burst of bombs,
pillage by gangs with guns and brooms,

hegemony of religious hoards
who run young women through with (s)words.

vi.

Why did you give your airplane in the war
my name? Were you obsessed before

I was a woman? Is that all
you ever thought? How hard that fall

by gravity onto your lap,
how (dis)tressing your lessons, that

display of bone and boxer shorts—
sex lessons of a sordid sort.

Your second marriage was a fine
amnesty. You never found mine

tolerable. Now that you're dead,
Daddy, (cold)cocked from heart to head,

I've moved on—safe to say—I'm all
in, my own (wo)man. *Que tal?*

vii.

*Adiós Papá. Su hija
está en Albuquerque.*

It's not so far from Roswell, where
that saucer crashed. I remember

how you walked me to the hangar
how we swooped over the (d)anger.

To me, at four, it looked less like
a flying saucer than a broken kite.

Wasn't I just your baby, then,
in the old days, at the war's end?

ABOUT THE COVER ARTIST

A former Associate Professor at Eastern Oregon University, **Terry Gloeckler** maintains research and outreach through university online teaching, gallery representation, exhibitions, visiting artist invitations, and residencies. She and Pamela taught in the Learning Community and offered together many Art & Writing classes at Eastern Oregon State College.

ABOUT THE AUTHOR

Pamela Yenser (BA WSU, MA PSU, MFA U of Idaho) is a creative nonfiction and poetry writer of witness. She is a 2nd-generation Kansan. Her Gove, Kansas, mother trained in Kansas City as a nurse and lived in "married" Pittsburg U. housing with a West Point pilot in flight training. Pamela was born during WWII in Alexandria, Virginia, at the home of her paternal grandparents. She attended grade through grad school in Wichita and Pittsburg, attributing early literary interests to Wichita SE High School teacher Lee Streiff (promoter of Beat poetry and aliens) and Iowa Workshop grads Michael Van Walleghen and Mark Costello, who joined Professor Bruce Cutler on the WSU creative writing faculty in the '60s. A winning debater/orator, Pamela was a contributing editor at *Mikrokosmos*, where she met native Kansas editor Jon Kelly Yenser. Pamela's awards include: 2020 poetry finalist at *Witness Magazine* for "Snow Angels" and NM Press Women NF/Folklore Prize for "Twilight at the Kimo Theatre"; 2019 award at W.B. Yeats Poetry Society of NY for "To Mary Shelley, Regarding Monsters," Ithaca Lit Difficult Fruit Prize for "Damn, *il Pleut*, and *Bosque* First-Place Poetry Prize for "Tenants of Greece." She's an Academy of American Poets Prize winner.

Author Links:
https://www.KansasPoets.com
https://www.nm-bookeditors.com/about
https://www.pw.org/directory/writers/Y?page=1

Praise for *CLOSE ENCOUNTERS Down Home*

"Everything abandoned comes alive" Pamela Yenser writes in *CLOSE ENCOUNTERS Down Home*, which becomes an invocation for resilience in a world filled with disaster at every turn: whether it's the wreckage of flying saucers in Roswell, or a brother and a mother who are irrevocably changed after a complicated birth, or an abusive father who is always in the driver's seat—whether it's by plane or car. Yenser does the difficult work of reckoning with trauma and the "family / history slamming the lid on truth." And though there's comfort in escape, and beauty to be found in the landscapes these poems traverse in a wide range of traditional and open poetic forms, Yenser reminds us "As long as you live / you won't forget," and there's danger everywhere. Lucky for us, we have a wonderful guide who knows her way around language and line, and is cunning enough to "have razor blades sewn / into the hem of every poem."

—**Gary Jackson**, author of *Missing You, Metropolis* (Graywolf Press, 2010), selected by Yusef Komunyakaa as winner of the 2009 Cave Canem Poetry Prize. He teaches in the MFA program at the College of Charleston in Charleston, South Carolina.

Pamela Yenser is a learned poet who knows the context, history, and texts of literature. Here she uses her supple and strict prosody to tell a family story about an abusive, daredevil father, a denying-praying mother, her "little retarded brother" ("She is her brother's keeper") and more. In airplanes and Airstream trailers "one catastrophe after another" happens to mark a childhood where "Visions of the devil / made you tithe, trade in the family silver." This astonishing chapbook delivers one revelation after another in poems exquisitely structured: "The past is a trap the Jaws of Life / can't break," she writes, "… but isn't this the work a poet is meant to do?" One poem in exact rhyming couplets is called "In the Garden of Demented Parents." Another, also in couplets, ends: "Look! I have razor blades sewn / into the hem of every poem." Read this brilliant and triumphant chapbook by a poet who limns the tragedy and triumph of her life.

—**Hilda Raz**, author of numerous poetry books, including *List & Story* (Stephen F. Austin U. Press, 2020) and *Letter from a Place I've Never Been, New and Collected Poems*, 1986-2020 (University of Nebraska Press, 2021).

Pamela Yenser's brave and tender poems spin together family history, personal resilience, and imaginative perseverance "sharp as that wreckage/ strewn like tinsel on glitter-/fields of tumbled rock" (as she writes in the title poem). Encompassing everything from a "bad weather balloon made of Kryptonite" to "a pineapple/ ruffled doily," Yenser juxtaposes the images and dreams of the otherworldly and the day-to-day life while also writing deeply of love and survival, monsters and angels, magic tricks and memories. This is a captivating and sparkling collection.

—**Caryn Mirriam-Goldberg**, Kansas Poet Laureate Emerita, author of *How Time Moves: New & Selected Poems* (Meadowlark Press, 2020).

Pamela Yenser's CLOSE ENCOUNTERS refers to, yes, the Roswell UFO, as well as family relationships that are a parallel encounter. The poems' narrator sees the flying saucer wreckage as a four-year-old. She writes about this iconic disruption of the skies as a way to reveal the workings of memory itself. This is an exciting personal fable that blends journalism, verse, and narration.

—**Denise Lowe**, author of *Shadow Light* (Red Mountain Press Award, 2018).

"Old Fruit of the Loom," Pamela Yenser writes of an abusive father. Also, please find a brain-damaged brother who pronounces death, "debt," and a mother in denial of it all, dazed by religion. Whether flying over wreckage of a flying saucer or driving down Route 66 in search of a neon sign of "a lady bent in two," this family does not travel well. In CLOSE ENCOUNTERS, Ms Yenser uses a dazzling array of forms to probe the dark corners of her subject. In the mode of Sylvia Plath, she mocks her nightmares, but goes beyond the so-called "Confessionals" to explore an entire culture of obsession. CLOSE ENCOUNTERS Down Home is a brave book by an expert writer who shines a light "because that's what poets do."

—**Murray Moulding**, a surrealist Colorado poet, and author of *Moon Over Easy* (Buzzard Press, 2009).

Pamela Yenser delves into the murky depths of familial tension and childhood mythology to uncover a wry history of UFOs, a father's questionable motives, and unexpected perspectives of the varied landscapes of Kansas and New Mexico. These poems are powered by succinct verses, apt metaphors, and surprising images that together weave a dynamic and irresistible collection that must be read again and again. CLOSE ENCOUNTERS Down Home is a brave book by an expert writer who shines a light "because that's what poets do."

—**Lisa Hase-Jackson**, author of *Flint & Fire* (Word Works, 2019).

The poems in Pamela Yenser's CLOSE ENCOUNTERS Down Home make a kind of memoir of growing up under the thumb of an abusive father and detached mother. They are disturbing poems in beautiful wrapping, sonically pleasing, vivid, and carefully crafted. The book's final poem, Damn, il pleut" is a masterful seven-section poem that leads readers from the speaker's infancy through the growing-up years and beyond, to the death of her father, when she is at last free. It's a bittersweet telling that begins and ends with a wish for a real father, someone he never managed to be; the final question's answer never comes, though by now readers know the answer never could have been a simple yes: "Wasn't I just your baby, then, in the old days, at the war's end?"

—**Rebecca Aronson**, author of *Anchor* (Orison Books, 2021), *Ghost Child of the Atalanta Bloom* (Winner of Orison Books Poetry Prize, 2016), and *Creature, Creature* (Winner of the Main-Traveled Roads Poetry Book Prize, 2007).

www.ingramcontent.com/pod-product-compliance
Lightning Source LLC
LaVergne TN
LVHW041552070426
835507LV00011B/1056